Charles Jones

Hernando de Soto

Charles Jones

Hernando de Soto

ISBN/EAN: 9783337147587

Printed in Europe, USA, Canada, Australia, Japan

Cover: Foto ©Andreas Hilbeck / pixelio.de

More available books at **www.hansebooks.com**

HERNANDO DE SOTO.

THE ADVENTURES ENCOUNTERED AND THE ROUTE PURSUED BY THE ADELANTADO
DURING HIS MARCH THROUGH THE TERRITORY EMBRACED WITHIN
THE PRESENT GEOGRAPHICAL LIMITS OF THE
STATE OF GEORGIA.

BY

CHARLES C. JONES, JR

[READ BEFORE THE GEORGIA HISTORICAL SOCIETY.]

PRINTED FOR THE AUTHOR.

J. H. ESTILL,
MORNING NEWS STEAM PRINTING HOUSE.
SAVANNAH, GA., 1880.

DE SOTO IN GEORGIA.

Flushed with the distinction he had won as a Captain in
Nicaragua, enriched by spoils gathered while a Lieutenant
General in the conquest of Peru, envious of the greater fame
of Pizarro, anxious to achieve victories grander and more
startling, and thirsting for booty more abundant, Hernando
De Soto sought and obtained from the Spanish Crown a
concession to subdue and settle all the region from the river
Palmas eastwardly to the "Island of Florida," including the
Tierra nueva adjoining it on the ocean.   Northwardly this
domain was without specific limit, and might be indefinitely
enlarged by discovery and occupancy.   Over it he was to
preside as Governor and Captain General, with the dignity
of Adelantado for life, and High Sheriff in perpetuity to
his heirs.

"For the purpose,"—so wrote the king,—"you will take
from these our kingdoms, and our said Indias, five hundred
men, with the necessary arms, horses, munitions, and military
stores ; and that you will go hence, from these our kingdoms,
to make the said conquest and settlement within a year first
following, to be reckoned from the day of the date of these
articles of authorization ; and that when you shall leave the
Island of Cuba to go upon that enterprise, you will take the
necessary subsistence for all that people during eighteen
months,—rather over than under that time,—entirely at your
cost and charges."   *   *   *

As great gain was anticipated, the Crown was careful to
reserve to itself, for the first six years, one-tenth of all gold
which should be realized from mines : and of that precious

metal, obtained by barter or as spoil during incursions, one-fifth was to be paid into the royal treasury.

Remembering the treasure trove in Peru, his Majesty was further pleased to enjoin that to his tribunal and exchequer should belong one-half of the gold, silver, stones, pearls, and other articles of value which might be taken from the graves, sepulchres, ocues, temples, religious precincts, public places, or private hoards of the natives.

To facilitate him in the subjugation and retention of this possession, and that he might the more easily command a convenient base of operations and supplies in the conduct of this great undertaking, De Soto was commissioned by the King, his master, Governor of Cuba.

Having, with much deliberation, selected and enlisted six hundred men, competent in every respect and thoroughly equipped, in April, 1538, the Adelantado set sail upon his mission. Passing over the bar of Sanlucar on Sunday,—the morning of Saint Lazarus,- he sought the open sea amid the braying of trumpets, the thunders of artillery, and the shouts of thousands. The expedition presented the aspect of a holiday excursion. Every heart on board was imbued with the spirit of adventure, confident of success, and per-suaded that the Land of Flowers would yield greater riches than the homes of the Incas. So general was the belief, entertained in Spain, of the wealth of the region, that the proudest of the land craved permission to be represented in the adventure either in person or by proxy. In the compo-sition of this band we find explanation of the spirit of en-durance and wonderful courage which characterized it during its eventful career.

On Pentecost De Soto arrived with his command in the harbor of Santiago, in Cuba of the Antilles, and thence pro-ceeded to Havana. Here he remained, perfecting his ar-rangements, until Sunday, the 18th of May, 1539; when, with a fleet of nine vessels,—five of them ships, two caravels, and two pinnaces,—he sailed for Florida. Delayed by contrary winds, it was not until the 25th, being the festival of *Espiritu Santo*, that land was descried and anchor cast a league from the shelving shore. On Friday, the 30th, the army debarked at a point two leagues from the town of the Indian chief Ucita Two hundred and thirteen horses were set on shore, the royal standard was elevated, and formal possession taken of *Terra Florida* in the name of Charles V. The camp was pitched upon the sands of Tampa Bay.

This was the most brilliant, enthusiastic, and warlike assemblage which, up to that period, had ever been seen this side the Atlantic. Herrera says De Soto had, of his private fortune, contributed one hundred thousand ducats for the equipment of this expedition. This little army was composed of men accustomed to wars, of personal daring, skilled in the use of weapons, and inured to hardships. Scarcely a gray head appeared among them. Their arms were strong, and their breasts filled with visions of glory and wealth. It was confidently believed that this new and unexplored Kingdom of Florida would exceed in riches the realms of Atahualpa, during the conquest of which De Soto had received, as his individual share of the spoils, the enormous sum of one hundred and eighty thousand crowns of gold.

Many of the young cavaliers who now rallied around this standard carried in their veins the best blood of Spain. Their equipment was superb and their enthusiasm unbounded. It was a strange sight, on the lonely shores of this new world, this convocation of soldiery in rich armor and costly dresses, of attending slaves, caparisoned horses, and burthen-bearing mules,—this assemblage of fleet greyhounds, savage blood-hounds, and grunting swine,—this accumulation of artillery, weapons, hand-cuffs, chains, neck-collars, crucibles for refining gold, tools, instruments, and material of every needed sort.

A valuable experience, acquired during the invasions of Nicaragua and Peru, was utilized on the present occasion; and the ample preparations made encouraged in the hearts of all hope of success more astounding than that which had characterized both those expeditions.

Twelve priests, eight clergymen of inferior rank, and four monks, accompanied the army. In the thirst for conquest and gold the conversion of the Aborigines was not forgotten. Men of letters, who were to perpetuate the events of the march, were also present.

With the wanderings of De Soto and his followers within the territorial limits of Florida, with the narrative of their battles with the natives, with the difficulties encountered in the crossing of rivers and the passage of perplexing morasses, with the sore disappointment experienced in the quest for gold and precious stones in this low-lying semi-tropical region, and with the accounts of the privations endured, we have now no special concern, as our inquiry is limited to a recital of what transpired within the confines of the present State of Georgia.

It may be stated, however, that after wintering at An-hayca, which was probably in the neighborhood of the modern town of Tallahassee,* De Soto, allured by a report of the existence of gold to the northward, determined to proceed in that direction in search for that much-coveted precious metal. Receiving an intimation that his march would extend for many leagues through a sparsely populated region, the Governor ordered his command to carry the

---

* Portions of Spanish armor have been exhumed in a field adjacent to this city, and other European relics have been found in this vicinity under circumstances confirming the suggestion here made.

largest allowance of maize. The cavalrymen packed a liberal supply of this grain on their horses, and the foot-soldiers conveyed as much as they could conveniently bear upon their backs. This store had been pillaged from the native villages, and the Indians, whom the Spaniards had forced to act as burden bearers during their previous wanderings and about the winter cantonment, had, in nakedness and chains, perished from hard usage. Sad is the record of the inhuman treatment meted out to the Aborigines by these Christian adventurers. Such was the utter contempt entertained for them by the Spaniards, that they hesitated not to subject them to every form of cruelty, humiliation, and privation. The men were condemned to the office of beasts of burden. The women were misued and driven from their habitations. Supplies of all sorts were ruthlessly appropriated. Even sepulchres were ransacked in the greedy search for pearls and hidden treasures. The path of the invader was marked on every hand by death, ruin, and desolation. The demoralizing influences exerted upon this aboriginal population by the inroads of the Spaniards cannot be overestimated.

On Wednesday, the 3d of March, 1540, the army moved northward, its objective point being Yupaha, governed by a woman, whose chief city was reported to be of astonishing size. Of some Indians captured in Napetuca, the treasurer, Juan Gaytan, had brought to camp a lad who spoke knowingly of this queen, of neighboring chiefs tributary to her, and of the clothing and gold with which they supplied her. So exactly did he describe the process of taking this metal from the earth, melting, and refining it, that the Spaniards came to the conclusion either that he had seen the whole affair with his own eyes, or that he had been taught of the Devil. Expectation was on tip-toe, and the belief was universal that the land of gold was at hand.

On the fourth day of its march the army encountered a
deep river, for the passage of which it became necessary to
construct a periagua. So swift was the current that a chain
was stretched from bank to bank for the guidance of this
craft. By this means the soldiers and the baggage were
crossed, and the horses directed in swimming the stream.
We believe this to have been the Ocklockony river. De
Soto had now arrived, or very nearly so, at the southwest
boundary of Georgia. Within the next forty-eight hours the
Indian village of Capachiqui was reached. At the approach
of the Spaniards the natives fled; but when five of the
Christians visited some Indian cabins, surrounded by a
thicket, in rear of the encampment, they were set upon by
Indians, lurking near, by whom one was killed and three
others were badly wounded. Pursued by a detachment from
the camp, the natives fled into a sheet of water filled with
forest trees, whither the cavalry could not follow them.
Thus does the Gentleman of Elvas record the death of the
first Spaniard who fell upon what is now the soil of Georgia.

Departing from Capachiqui on the 11th, and traversing a
desert, the expedition had, on the 21st, penetrated as far as
Toalli. This region, which the historian designates as a
desert, was doubtless a dreary pine barren, devoid of population and but little frequented by any animal life. The site
of Toalli or Otoa cannot now be definitely ascertained; but,
as it was near Achese, or Ochis, (which, according to Mr.
Gallatin, is the Muskhoge name of the Ocmulgee river,) we
may not greatly err in locating it somewhere in Irwin, or
Coffee county.

Of the peculiarities of this place the Gentleman of Elvas,
whose narrative, in the main, we adopt, has perpetuated the
following impressions: The houses of this town were different from those behind, which were covered with dry grass.
Thenceforward they were roofed with cane after the fashion

of tile. They are kept very clean. Some have their sides so made of clay as to look like tapia. Throughout the cold country every Indian has a winter house plastered inside and out, with a very small door which is closed at dark, and, a fire being made within, it remains heated like an oven, so that clothing is not needed during the night time. He has likewise a house for summer, and near it a kitchen where fire is made and bread baked. Maize is kept in barbacoa, which is a house with wooden sides, like a room, raised aloft on four posts. It has a floor of cane. The houses of the principal men, besides being larger than those of the common people, had deep balconies in front, furnished with benches made of the swamp cane. Adjacent were large barbacoas in which were collected maize, the skins of deer, and the blankets of the country, offered as tribute by the populace. These blankets resembled shawls, and were fashioned from the inner bark of trees, and from a certain grass which, when beaten, yielded a flax-like fibre.* They were used by the women as coverings. One was worn about the body from the waist downward. Another was thrown over the shoulders, leaving the right arm free after the manner of the Gypsies. The men were content with one, which was carried in like manner over the shoulders. The loins were covered with a bragueiro of deer skin, after the fashion of the woolen breech-cloth once customary in Spain. These blankets were colored either vermilion or black. Garments of well-dressed deer skin were also in vogue, and shoes made of the same material.

Three days were spent at Toalli: and, on Saturday, the 24th of March, the expedition moved onward. Thursday evening, while crossing a small stream over which a bridge had been thrown for the passage of the command, Benito Fernandes, a Portuguese, was drowned. A short distance

* This was evidently the tough *silk grass* of the region.

beyond this stream was located the village of Achese, whose inhabitants, upon the approach of the Europeans, plunged into the river and made their escape. Among some captives taken was found one who understood the language spoken by the Indian who had acted in the capacity of guide to Yupaha. By him the Governor sent a message to the chief, dwelling on the further side of the river, desiring an interview with him. Responding to the invitation, the Cacique appeared with words of courtesy and an avowal of friendship. Frankly thanking him for his good will, De Soto informed him that he was the child of the Sun,* coming from his abode, and that he was seeking the greatest prince and the richest province. The Chief replied that further on there reigned a powerful King whose territory was called Ocute. A guide, who understood the language of this province, having been furnished, the captives were set at liberty. Before leaving Toalli a high wooden cross was erected in the middle of the town-yard, and some effort made to instruct the natives in the doctrines of Christianity.

Resuming his march on the first of April, De Soto moved along a river whose shores were thickly populated. On the fourth day he passed through the town of Altamaca, and on the tenth arrived at Ocute. If we are correct in our impression, the march of the expedition had been in a northeasterly direction, and the Spaniards were now probably in Laurens county. In the word Altamaca [or *Altapaha* as it is written by Biedma and also by Garcilasso de la Vega] we recognize one of the prominent rivers in Southern Georgia, and the many traces of early constructive skill, ancient relic beds, and old Indian fields along the line of that, and of the Oconee river, give ample token that in former times the abo-

---

* This announcement, if credited, was calculated to make a profound impression upon the natives, as the Florida Tribes, in the sixteenth century, were nearly all *Sun-worshippers.*

riginal population cormorant here was by no means inconsiderable.

While approaching Ocute, De Soto's command was met
by two thousand Indians bearing, as a present from
the Chief, many conies, partridges, bread made of maize,
dogs, and two turkeys. Such was the scarcity of meat that
the Spaniards welcomed this offering of dogs as heartily as
if it had been a gift of fat sheep. In the language of the
narrative from which we have quoted so freely : " Of flesh
meat and salt in many places and many times there had
been great need ; and they were so scarse that if a man fell
sicke there was nothing to cherish him withall ; and with a
sicknesse that in another place easilie might have been rem-
edied, he consumed away till nothing but skinne and bones
was left : and they died of pure weaknes, some of them saying ; 'If I had a slice of meate or a few cornes of salt, I
should not die.' "

The sufferings of these Spaniards were grievous and
almost without interruption. On more than one occasion
they were on the point of starving when relieved by the
generous offerings of the natives. Surely these primitive
inhabitants were hospitable peoples. In view of the harsh
treatment dealt out to them by the whites we are little less
than amazed at such exhibitions of charity and good will.

While the Indians, through the apt use of their bows and
arrows, supplied themselves abundantly with game, the
Spaniards, less expert with their clumsy weapons, and on the
march not daring to straggle, so craved meat that upon their
entrance into a native village they at once set about killing
every dog in sight. Should the private soldier, who had
been so fortunate as to secure one of these animals, omit to
send his Captain a quarter, he would surely be visited with
displeasure and extra duty.

Having obtained from the Cacique of Ocute four hundred

tamemes, or burden bearers, the Governor, on the twelfth of April, took his departure. Passing through Cofaqui he journeyed to Patofa, by the Mico of which he was hospitably entreated.

While here the Indian youth, who had accompanied De Soto as his guide and interpreter, "began to froth at the mouth, and threw himself on the ground as if he were possessed of the Devil." An exorcism having been said over him, however, the fit went off : at least so runs the story.

Upon the Cacique of Patofa a contribution was levied of seven hundred tamemes and a four days' supply of maize. Thus aided, the expedition started, apparently in a north-easterly direction, following a path which gradually grew less and less distinct, until, at the end of the sixth day, all trace was lost in the midst of a wide-spreading pine barren. For three days more vainly seeking to acquire some valuable information, and having marched continuously, the Governor called a halt and went into camp among the pine trees. During these nine days he had with difficulty forded two rivers, [sources of the Great Ogeechee ?] and swam another. [Briar Creek ?]

Accompanied by some cavalry and infantry, De Soto made a detour of some five or six leagues, looking for a path. He returned at night, having failed to find any inhabitants, quite dejected and sore perplexed. His command was in a sorry plight. The circumjacent country was a barren. No sign of human habitation appeared. The maize which his soldiers had brought from Patofa was utterly consumed. Both beasts and men were lean and hungry. In this enfeebled condition resistance, in the event of an attack, seemed impossible. Starvation and annihilation stared the expedition in the face. Unable longer to subsist the burthen bearers from Patofa, they were dismissed to make their way back to their homes as best they could.

The next day, intent upon extricating himself from this perilous situation, the Governor sent out four expeditions,— each consisting of a captain and eight cavalrymen,—with instructions to scour the country and find some source of relief, some avenue of escape. The day was consumed in a fruitless search, and they all came into camp at night-fall leading their broken-down horses, or driving them before them. On the following day, having selected the best horses, and soldiers who could swim, he organized four bands, each containing eight mounted men. Baltasar de Gallegos, who commanded one, was directed to move up the river. Juan de Anasco, with another, was to move downwards. Alfonso Romo and Juan Rodrigues Lobillo, with the other two, were ordered to strike into the country.

The thirteen sows which had been brought from Cuba had so multiplied during the progress of the expedition, that there were now three hundred swine in camp. During this season of privation these animals were killed and a ration of a half pound of fresh pork was issued, per diem, to each man. This, supplemented by such native herbs as could be collected and boiled, constituted the only subsistence of the soldiery. Upon the rough grass, leaves, and the tops of palmettos, did the horses feed. The entire command was in an enfeebled, dispirited, and almost perishing condition.

On Sunday afternoon [April 25th] Juan de Anasco, who was in charge of one of these reconnoitering parties, returned, bringing a woman and a youth whom he had captured. He reported that at a remove of some twelve or thirteen leagues he had found a small town. At this intelligence, says the Gentleman of Elvas, the Governor and his people were as much delighted as if they had been raised from death to life.

Without awaiting the incoming of the other detachments, De Soto set out for this village, which the Indians called

Aymay, and to which the Spaniards gave the name of So-
corro.* At the foot of a tree in the camp was buried a letter
stating in what direction the command would march. That
the attention of the absentees on their return might be
called to it, on the bark of the tree were cut, with a hatchet,
these words : "Dig here : at the foot of this pine you will
find a letter."

Following the road which Anasco had made while passing
through the woods, the Governor set out on the morning of
the 26th of April, taking with him his troopers who were
best mounted, and moved as rapidly as he could in the direction of Aymay. That village he reached before night-fall.
The army followed, as best it could in its enfeebled condition, straggling all the way. At this town a barbacoa of
parched meal and maize was found, the contents of which
were immediately issued to the starving command.

Four Indians were captured who refused to give any information touching the existence of any adjacent native
villages. One of them having been burnt, another stated
that at a remove of two days' journey was the province of
Cutifachiqui.

Two days afterward the three captains arrived with their
detachments. On returning to camp they found the buried
letter and followed on in the trail left by the army. Two
soldiers remained behind, and they belonged to the detachment of Juan Rodriguez. Their horses had entirely given
out and they lagged with them. After a severe reprimand
from the Governor, this officer was dispatched to hurry up
these loiterers. Without tarrying for their coming, De Soto
advanced in the direction of Cutifachiqui. On his journey
thitherward three Indians were taken who informed the
Spaniards that the Queen of that province had been advised
of the approach of the army and, in her chief town, was

* Village of *Good Relief.*

awaiting the arrival of the strangers. One of them was immediately dispatched with a message of friendship from the Governor to the Cacica, and the announcement that he would speedily visit her. Upon the Governor's arrival at the river, four canoes approached from the opposite bank. In one of these was a kinswoman of the Cacica who had been by her deputed to extend an invitation to the Spaniards to cross over and partake of the hospitalities of the town. She excused the absence of the Cacica on the ground that she was engaged in giving directions for the reception of such distinguished guests. She returned with the thanks of the Governor. Soon after the Cacica came out of the village, seated in a chair of state,* which was borne by some of the principal men to the water's edge. Thence alighting, she entered a canoe, the stern of which was sheltered by an awning. Cushions lay extended in the bottom, and upon these she reclined. In her passage across the river she was accompanied by her chief men and other subjects in canoes. Having landed, she approached the spot where De Soto awaited her, and addressed him with courteous words of welcome. Drawing from over her head a long string of pearls she suspended it about the Governor's neck in token of amity. She also presented him with many shawls and dressed skins, constituting the clothing of her country. Finely formed, with great beauty of countenance, and possessing much native grace and dignity, the Spaniards were impressed by her appearance and queenly conduct. During her interview with the Governor she sat upon a stool carried by one of her attendants. Her subjects preserved an unbroken silence and most respectful demeanor. She was the

---

* In Plate xxxvii. of the " Brevis Narratio " we have a spirited illustration of the litter, or palanquin, in which the queens of these primitive peoples were conveyed.

See also Jones' *Antiquities of the Southern Indians*, p. 72. New York. 1873.

first female ruler whom De Soto had met during all his wanderings. The Governor was sensibly moved by her generous
salutation and pleasing behavior. In acknowledgment of
her beautiful gift, and as a pledge of peace and friendship,
De Soto, drawing from his finger a ring of gold set with a
ruby, gently placed it upon one of her fingers. The hospitalities of her town were generously extended. She promised
to share her store of maize with the strangers, and said that
she would send canoes for their conveyance to the other
side of the river. This ceremony of welcome ended, the
Cacica returned to her home. On the following day, in
canoes and upon rafts furnished by the natives, the army
crossed to the further shore and found food and rest in wig-
wams shaded by luxuriant mulberry trees. Four horses
were drowned in the passage of the river. So soon as De
Soto was lodged in the village many wild turkeys were sent
to him, and during his sojourn in this place he and his men
were entertained with every mark of hospitality. To be
thus rested and feasted was most joyous to this band, foot-
sore and weary, diappointed, dejected, and well nigh over-
borne by the difficulties and privations of the journey.

The inhabitants, well proportioned and of a good countenance, were more civilized than all other peoples seen in the
wide-extended territory of Florida. They wore clothing and
shoes. The country, in that early spring time, was beautiful,
and gave every indication of fertility. The temperature was
delightful, and the woods were most attractive. The Spaniards were particularly gratified with the profusion of walnut
and mulberry trees. To all, save the Governor, it seemed good
to form a permanent settlement here. The point appeared
favorable for raising supplies; and, as the natives stated it
was only two days' journey from the coast, it was thought
that ships from New Spain, Peru, Saucta Marta, and Tierra-
Firme, going to Spain, might be induced to stop here and

refresh their crews. Thus ignorant were these strangers of their true geographical position.

In the vicinity of Cutifachiqui were large, vacant towns overgrown with grass. It was ascertained that two years before there had been a pest in the land; and, in order to escape its ravages, multitudes of the inhabitants had removed to other localities.

In the barbacoas were found "large quantities of clothing, shawls of thread made from the bark of trees, and others of feathers, white, gray, vermilion, and yellow, rich and proper for winter. There were also many well-dressed deer-skins, of colors drawn over with designs, of which had been made shoes, stockings and hose."

Upon searching the sepulchres in the town three hundred and fifty weight of pearls, and figures of babies and birds made from iridescent shells, were taken from them. The suggestion of the Spanish narrators is that this quest was undertaken by permission of the Cacica, who observed how highly the Christians valued these gems of the water. When we remember, however, how ardently attached these primitive peoples were to the graves of their dead, how carefully they deposited in them the treasures of the deceased, how tenderly they watched over and sacredly guarded the last resting-places of their departed, we recognize in this procedure not the voluntary intervention of the native, but the cupidity, the violence, and the outrage of the foreigner.

In the town were found a dirk and beads of European manufacture. From the best information which could be gathered touching their origin and the manner in which the Indians became possessed of them, it was believed that they had been obtained from some members of the unfortunate expedition of the Governor-licentiate Ayllon. Biedma says, in alluding to these relics, "We found buried two wood axes of Castilian make, a rosary of jet beads, and some false pearls such as are taken from this country [Spain] to traffic with the Indians, all of which we supposed they got in exchange made with those who followed the Licentiate Ayllon. From the information given by the Indians, the sea should be about thirty leagues distant. We knew that the people who came with Ayllon hardly entered the country at all : that they remained continually on the coast until his sickness and death. In strife for command, they then commenced to kill each other, while others of them died of hunger; for one, whose lot it was to have been among them, told us that of six hundred men who landed, only fifty-seven escaped,—a loss caused to a great extent by the wreck of a big ship they had brought, laden with stores."

Learning that the mother of the Cacica resided about twelve leagues down the river, and that she was a widow, De Soto expressed a strong desire to see her. This wish was doubtless born of the fact that she was reported to be the owner of many valuable pearls. Upon intimating his pleasure, the Cacica of Cutifachiqui dispatched twelve of her prominent subjects to entreat her mother to come and see the wonderful strangers and the remarkable animals they had brought with them. To these messengers the widow administered a severe rebuke, declined to accompany them, and returned to her daughter words condemnatory of her conduct. Still intent upon his object, De Soto dispatched Juan de Anasco, with thirty companions, to secure the presence of the queen mother. They were accompanied by a youthful warrior whom the Cacica selected as a guide. He was a near relative of the widow and had been reared by her. It was supposed that he of all others could best secure for the expedition a favorable reception. In the blush of early manhood he possessed handsome features, and a graceful, vigorous form. "His head was decorated with lofty plumes of different colored feathers; he wore a mantle of

dressed deer-skin; in his hand he bore a beautiful bow so
highly varnished as to appear as if finely enameled; and at
his shoulder hung a quiver full of arrows. With a light, and
elastic step, and an animated and gallant air, his whole appearance was that of an ambassador worthy of the young
and beautiful princess whom he served."

What next befell the Spanish captain and his Indian guide
we relate in the language of Theodore Irving, quoting from
Herrera.

"Juan de Anasco and his comrades having proceeded
nearly three leagues, stopped to make their mid-day meal,
and take their repose beneath the shade of some wide-
spreading trees, as the heat was oppressive. The Indian
guide had proved a cheerful and joyous companion, enter-
taining them all the way with accounts of the surrounding
country and the adjacent provinces. On a sudden, after
they had halted he became moody and thoughtful, and,
leaning his cheek upon his hand, fell into a reverie, uttering
repeated and deep-drawn sighs. The Spaniards noticed his
dejection, but, fearing to increase it, forebore to demand the
cause.

"After a time he quietly took off his quiver, and placing
it before him, drew out the arrows slowly one by one. They
were admirable for the skill and elegance with which they
were formed. Their shafts were reeds. Some were tipped
with buck's horn, wrought with four corners like a diamond;
some were pointed with the bones of fishes, curiously fashioned; others with barbs of the palm and other hard woods;
and some were three pronged. They were feathered in a
triangular manner, to render their flight of greater accuracy.
The Spaniards could not sufficiently admire their beauty;
they took them up and passed them from hand to hand, ex-
amining and praising their workmanship and extolling the
skill of their owner. The youthful Indian continued

thoughtfully emptying his quiver, until, almost at the last, he drew forth an arrow with a point of flint, long and sharp, and shaped like a dagger; then, casting round a glance, and seeing the Spaniards engaged in admiring his darts, he suddenly plunged the weapon in his throat, and fell dead upon the spot.

"Shocked at the circumstance, and grieved at not having been able to prevent it, the Spaniards called to their Indian attendants and demanded the reason of this melancholy act in one who had, just before, been so joyous.

"The Indians broke into loud lamentations over the corpse; for the youth was tenderly beloved by them, and they knew the grief his untimely fate would cause to both their princesses. They could only account for his self-destruction by supposing him perplexed and afflicted about his embassy. He knew that his errand would be disagreeable to the mother, and apprehended that the plan of the Spaniards was to carry her off. He alone knew the place of her concealment, and it appeared to his generous mind an unworthy return for her love and confidence thus to betray her to strangers. On the other hand he was aware, that should he disobey the mandates of his young mistress, he would lose her favor and fall into disgrace. Either of these alternatives would be worse than death; he had chosen death, therefore, as the lesser evil, and as leaving to his mistress a proof of his loyalty and devotion.

"Such was the conjecture of the Indians, to which the Spaniards were inclined to give faith. Grieving over the death of the high-minded youth they mournfully resumed their journey.

"They now, however, found themselves at a loss about the road. None of the Indians knew in what part of the country the widow was concealed,—the young guide who had killed himself being alone master of the secret. For the rest of

that day and until the following noon they made a fruitless
search, taking prisoners some natives who all professed utter
ignorance on the subject. Juan de Anasco being a fleshy
man and somewhat choleric, was almost in a fever with the
vexation of his spirit, the weight of his armor, and the heat
of the day; he was obliged, however, to give up the quest
after the widow, and to return to the camp much mortified
at having for once failed in an enterprise."

Three days afterward, upon the offer of an Indian to
guide him, by water, to the point where the widow had se-
creted herself, Anasco, with twenty companions, departed in
two canoes for the purpose of capturing her. At the end of
six days he returned vexed and chagrined at the failure of
his expedition. Thus did the queen's mother avoid the
Spaniards and preserve her pearls.

Still intent upon his quest for gold, in response to his inquiries De Soto was told that there was here yellow, and
also white metal, similar to that shown by the Spaniards.
Natives were dispatched to bring samples of both. To the
sore disappointment of the Christians, however, the yellow
metal proved to be a copper ore, and the white metal a light
crumbling material like mica.

Turning his attention again to the pearls of the region, the
Governor visited Talomeco, the former chief town of the
province, distant about a league from the village of the Princess of Cutifachiqui, where was a large mausoleum containing many dead and a large store of pears. On this occasion
he was accompanied by Anasco,—the contador, or royal ac-
countant of the expedition,—by the officers of the royal
revenue, and by a number of his principal officers and
soldiers.

The main edifice at Talomeco is described as being one
hundred paces in length, and forty in breadth, with lofty
roofs of reed. At its entrance were posted gigantic statues

of wood, carved with no inconsiderable skill, the largest
being twelve feet high. Armed with various weapons, they
maintained threatening attitudes and exhibited ferocious as-
pects. The interior of the temple was filled with statues of
various sizes and shapes, and with a great profusion of
conchs and different kinds of marine and fluviatile shells.

"Around the sepulchre were benches on which were
wooden chests, skillfully wrought, but without locks or
hinges. In these were the bodies of the departed caciques
and chieftains of Cutifachiqui left to their natural decay.   *
*   *   Besides these chests there were smaller ones, and
baskets wrought of cane, which were filled with valuable
furs, and Indian robes of dressed skins, and mantles made
of the inner rind and bark of trees, and others of a species
of grass, which, when beaten, was not unlike flax. There
were others formed with feathers of various colors, which
the natives wore during the winter. But above all, they
contained pearls of every size and in incredible quantities,
together with the figures of children and birds made of
pearl. The Portuguese narrator says they obtained fourteen
bushels of pearls, and that the female Cacique assured them
that if they searched the neighboring villages they might
find enough to load all the horses of the army. Nor is the
Inca less extravagant in his account." Biedma says : " We
took from it " [the mosque] " a quantity of pearls of the
weight of as many as six arrobas and a half, or seven,
though they were injured from lying in the earth and in the
adipose substance of the dead."

While the existence of pearls upon the persons and in the
graves of the natives of this region may not be questioned,
it is highly probable that the accounts of the quantities of
these glistening beads here found are exaggerated. The
treasures of the New World were greatly magnified by these
adventurers, who dealt largely in the marvelous, and sought,

by glowing descriptions, to excite the wonder and enlist the sympathies of their friends at home.

Shell heaps,—still extant along the line of southern rivers, upon the shores of ponds and lakes, and on the sea coast,— are not infrequent. Upon the animals which they contained did the Aborigines depend in no small degree for food, and the pearls thence obtained were industriously gathered and perforated to be worn as ornaments. Through aboriginal trade relations constant supplies were also procured from margatiferous shells of the Gulf of Mexico.*

It was the purpose of the intendants of the revenue, who accompanied the expedition, to collect and preserve all the pearls found in these temples and graves, but upon a suggestion by the Governor that they could not conveniently be carried, and that at present they were simply engaged in an expedition for discovery, it was resolved that specimens only should be taken for exhibition in Havana, and that the rest should remain until such time as they might return and possess the land. Handfuls of large pearls were distributed among the officers, with an exhortation from De Soto that they make rosaries of them, and the Crown officers were allowed to retain quite a quantity which they had already weighed out.

Adjacent to the great sepulchre were several buildings which served as armories. In them were deposited weapons of various kinds. They were under the charge of attendants who carefully watched and kept them in admirable order.

So pleased were the soldiers with this goodly land, with its fruits and stores of pearls, that they urged upon the Governor the propriety of forming here a permanent settlement. But, in the language of the Gentleman of Elvas,

---

* In further proof of the general use of pearls, as ornaments, among the Southern Tribes, see Jones' *Antiquities of the Southern Indians*, etc. Chapter XXI. New York. 1873.

"The Governor, since his intent was to seeke another treasure like that of Atabalipa, lord of Peru, was not contented
with a good countrie, nor with pearles, though many of them
were worth their weight in gold. And if the countrie had
been divided among the Christians, those which the Indians
had fished for afterward would have been of more value; for
those which they had, because they burned them in the fire,
did leese their colour. The Governour answered them that
urged him to inhabit, that in all the countrie there were not
victuals to sustaine his men one moneth, and that it was
needfull to resort to the port of Ocus, where Maldonado was
to stay for them; and that if no richer countrie were found,
they might returne againe to that whensoever they would;
and in the meantime the Indians would sow their fields, and
it would be better furnished with maiz.

"He inquired of the Indians whether they had notice of
any great lord farther into the land. They told him that
twelve daies journie from thence there was a province called
Chiaha, subject to the lord of Coça. Presently the Governour determined to seeke that land. And being a sterne
man, and of few words, though he was glad to sift and know
the opinion of all men, yet after hee had delivered his owne
hee would not be contraried, and alwaies did what liked
himselfe, and so all men did condescend unto his will. And
though it seemed an errour to leave that countrie (for others
might have been sought round about, where the people
might have been sustained untill the harvest had been
readie there, and the maiz gathered), yet there was none
that would say anything against him after they knew his
resolution."

We have thus traced the progress of the expedition from
the southern confines of Georgia to the mulberry shaded
town of Cutifachiqui. The general trend of the march was
northeast, with manifestly many deflections which we have

found it impossible to pursue with any degree of accuracy.* From Anhayca to the point where the army is now resting the route has been, in our judgment, nearly parallel with the Atlantic coast. We believe the location of Cutifachiqui to have been identical with that of Silver Bluff, on the left bank of the Savannah river, about twenty-five miles by water below the city of Augusta. The river here impinges against a bold bluff, rising some thirty-five feet above the level of the adjacent swamp, and extending along the line of the stream, with an unbroken front, for the distance of nearly a mile. Bounding this high ground on the west is Hollow Creek. Stretching to the north is fertile upland. At this place were extensive Indian fields when the region was first visited and settled by Europeans. Three miles below, in a direct line, is another bluff upon the same side of the Savannah river,—not quite as bold as that where we now stand,— with an adjacent expanse of rich upland, which we suppose to be the site of Talomeco. Here also were old Indian fields, and manifest tokens of primitive occupancy.

When, one hundred and three years ago, [April, 1776,] William Bartram visited Silver Bluff,†—then owned by

---

* That the progress of the expedition was necessarily slow will be freely admitted when it is remembered that it was traversing the depths of an unbroken, pathless forest permeated at irregular intervals by rivers, streams and swamps,— that its baggage and supplies were transported upon the backs of the soldiers and of Indian burthen-bearers, and that a drove of hogs kept pace with the march.

† Four years afterward [1780], to the history of this somewhat famous locality was added a chapter whose incidents furnish a bright illustration of those partizan adventures and patriotic exploits which characterized the conduct of the Southern campaign during the war of the Revolution.

The annual royal present for the Indians, consisting of powder, ball, small arms, liquor, salt, blankets and other articles of which the impoverished Continentals stood sadly in need was, in May of that year, on deposit here, awaiting distribution. Two companies of infantry, detached from Colonel Brown's forces in Augusta, were then stationed in the stockade fort at this point, known as Fort Galphin, to guard this present. Made aware of this fact through the vigilance of his scouts, carefully concealing his movement, and leaving his artillery

George Galphin, the famous Indian trader,—there were still extant " various monuments and vestiges of the residence of the ancients : as Indian conical mounts, terraces, areas, etc., as well as remains or traces of fortresses of regular formation, as if constructed after the modes of European military architects, which are supposed to be ancient camps of the Spaniards who formerly fixed themselves at this place in hopes of finding silver."

These proofs of early constructive skill have, however, all disappeared. They have been obliterated by the ploughshare and the changing seasons, and the most marked of them, occupying positions near the edge of the bluff, have been swept away by the encroaching tides of the tawny-hued

and the tired of his battalion under the command of Colonel Eaton, Lieutenant Colonel Henry Lee determined to press forward at once and secure these much coveted supplies for the American camp. Mounting a detachment of infantry behind his dragoons, by a forced march and unperceived by the enemy, on the 21st of May, 1780, he halted his panting squadrons beneath the pines which skirted the field in which Fort Galphin stood. The day was excessively sultry, and men and animals were so oppressed by heat and overcome by thirst that his little column was for the time incapable of further exertion.

After a short rest Colonel Lee directed his dismounted militiamen to make, unobserved, the circuit of the fort, and to attack it from a point opposite to that which he then occupied. This strategy was invoked under the impression that the garrison would be enticed from the fort in their pursuit, and that thus the capture of the post by a rapid assault under his immediate supervision would be ensured beyond peradventure. As was anticipated, so soon as the militiamen debouched from the woods the garrison flew to arms and, rushing from the fort, proceeded to drive them away. Feebly resisting at first, they quickly retired before their pursuers, their retreat being covered by some cavalry previously disposed for that purpose. At this juncture a rapid advance under Captain Rudolph was ordered, and the assaulting column easily gained possession of the fort.

In the language of the author of the " Memoirs of the War in the Southern Department,"* " the garrison, with the valuable deposit in its safe keeping, gave a rich reward for our toils and sufferings."

The foundations of the old brick house which formed the residence of George Galphin, and which witnessed the prowess of the gallant Colonel of Cavalry and his brave troopers on that sultry May morning, may still be seen.

* Vol. II., p. 89 et seq.
See also Jones' "Antiquities of the Southern Indians," p. 151 et seq.

Savannah. During the memory of an old inhabitant, more than one hundred feet in breadth of this bluff have been eaten away and dissipated by the insatiate currents of this river. That the Spaniards were once here, was generally believed at the period of Bartram's visit, and the tradition has been handed down to the present day. But our intelligent traveller was manifestly at fault in ascribing some of these earthworks to the agency of Europeans. So far as we can discover, De Soto fortified no camps within the present limits of Georgia and left no enduring proofs of his occupancy.

The presence of pyrites and of sulphurous nodules in the face of the bluff, and frequent particles and flakes of mica still attest the sources from which the Indians, in the days of De Soto, attempted to satisfy the Spanish craving for gold and silver. While it may be true that nuggets of native silver have been here found, as is stoutly asserted by some, the suggestion that this bluff derived its name from this circumstance we deem quite improbable. We would rather ascribe the name to the tradition, derived from the Indians, and dominant here at the period of primal settlement, that many years before a band of white men had here come and, in the bed of the river and elsewhere in the neighborhood, made search for this metal.

Those who have studied the route of De Soto are not agreed as to the precise location of Cutifachiqui. Thus, Dr. Monette places it on the peninsula formed by the confluence of the Broad and Savannah rivers. Dr. McCulloh thinks it was on the Ocmulgee river, in Monroe county. William Bartram, Colonel Albert James Pickett, Mr. Albert Gallatin, Mr. William B. Rye, Mr. Buckingham Smith, and Mr. J. Carson Brevoort all incline to the belief that at Silver Bluff we behold the site of the ancient village of Cutifachiqui. In this impression we sympathize. Mr. Theodore Irving, too, appears to yield to this persuasion, while freely confessing how perplexing it is to "make out the route in conformity to modern landmarks."

During the latter portion of the Spanish sojourn at Cutifachiqui the Queen had become so much incensed at the outrages perpetrated by the Christians upon her subjects, that when advised by De Soto of his contemplated deparparture, she utterly refused to furnish him with guides and tamemes. The Governor thereupon placed her under guard; and, upon commencing his journey northward on the third day of May, he compelled her, on foot, escorted by her female attendants, to accompany him. Commenting upon this conduct of De Soto the Gentleman of Elvas remarks: This was not "so good usage as she deserved for the good wil she shewed and good entertainement that she had made him. And he verified that old proverb which saith: 'For weldoing I receive evil.'" The present objective point of the expedition was Guaxule, situated near the northerly or northwesterly confines of the territory ruled over by the Cacica of Cutifachiqui. As her domains were quite extensive, De Soto trusted, through her presence and influence, to control the natives along the line of his march. In this expectation he was not disappointed. "In all the townes where the Governour passed, the ladie commanded the Indians to come and carrie the burdens from one towne to another. We passed through her countrie an hundred leagues, in which, as we saw, she was much obeyed. For the Indians did all that she commanded them with great efficacie and diligence." Before departing from Cutifachiqui the army was organized into two divisions, the one commanded by the Adelantado in person, and the other under the guidance of Baltazar de Gallegos. Upon the second day the Spaniards encountered a storm of wind, lightning, and hail, so severe that, had they not sought the close protection of the forest trees, many of them would have perished. The hail-stones were as large as pigeon's eggs.*

After a march of seven days the Province of Chelaque was reached. In this name, with but slight alteration, we recognize the land of the Cherokees. According to Adair and others the national name was derived from Chee-ra—"*fire*." Hence Cherakees,—Chelakees, Cherokees.

The route had thus far, if we understand it aright, been upward and along the right bank of the Savannah river. De Soto was now, we think, within the confines of the present county of Franklin. The country was described as "the poorest off for maize" of any which had thus far been seen in Florida. The inhabitants were domestic, slight of form, and, at that season, quite naked. Upon the roots of plants dug in the forests, and upon the animals destroyed with their arrows, did they chiefly subsist. One of the chiefs presented the Governor with two deer-skins as a mark of friendship. Turkeys abounded. In one village seven hundred of these birds were given to the Spaniards; and there was no scarcity of them in other localities.

Five days were occupied in passing from this province to Xualla. The chief town of this last named province bore the same name, and was located on the flanks of a mountain with a small but rapid river flowing near. We venture the suggestion that this village was situated in Nacoochee valley, Habersham county, and that the mountain referred to was Yonah. In this valley physical proofs of primitive occupancy are still extant, and metallic fragments of European manufacture have there been found confirmatory of the fact that many years prior to the settlement of this region by the whites, it had been visited by kindred peoples. We do not now allude to the remains of an ancient village,—the cabins

* Herrera.

of which were made of logs hewn and notched by means of chopping axes,—unearthed by Colonels Merriwether and Lumsden in Duke's Creek valley in 1834, or to the traces of early mining in Valley River valley, and adjacent localities, where deep shafts passing through gneiss rock,—their sides scarred by the impression of sharp tools,—and windlasses of post-oak with cranks and gudgeon holes were observed,— the tree< growing above this old settlement and springing from the mouths and sides of these abandoned pits being not less than two hundred years old. These are to be re'erred to the labors of Tristan de Luna, who, in 1560, at the command of Louis de Velasco, came with three hundred Spanish soldiers into this region, and spent the summer in eager and laborious search for gold. This expedition moved up from Pensacola, and was dispatched on the faith of the representations, made by returned soldiers from De Soto's command, of the presence of the precious metal among these mountains. We are informed by the German traveller, Johannes Lederer, that as late as 1669 and 1670 the Spaniards were employed in working gold and silver mines in the Appalachian mountains.

Although little grain was found at Xualla, the Adelantado rested there two days that he might refresh his weary soldiers and recuperate his horses which were lean and sadly jaded.

Apparently inclining his route westwardly, De Soto set out for Guaxule, which marked the furthest confines, in that direction, of the dominion of the Queen of Cutifachiqui. During this stage of the journey the Queen succeeded in making her escape into the forests. So thoroughly did she conceal herself, that efforts for her recapture proved fruitless. We are told by the Fidalgo of Elvas that she took with her a cane box, like a small trunk, called *petaca*, full of unbored pearls of great value. Up to the moment of her flight this precious box

had been borne by one of her female attendants. The
Governor permitted this, hoping that when he reached
Guaxule,—at which point he was minded to liberate her,—
he would be able to beg these pearls of her. In her return
homewards she was accompanied by three slaves who de-
serted from the camp. A horseman, named Alimamos, who
had been left behind sick of a fever, came upon these slaves
and persuaded two of them to abandon their evil design.
The third, however,—a slave of André de Vasconcelos,—
remained with the Cacica. When Alimamos last saw them,
they were living together as man and wife, and were together
to return to Cutifachiqui. Such is the last glimpse we have
of this Indian Queen whose welcome of and association with
De Soto form one of the marked episodes in the nebulous
story of this wonderful expedition.

The country traversed during the five days consumed in
marching from Xualla to Guaxule was mountainous, with
intervening valleys "rich in pasturage and irrigated by clear
and rapid streams." Much fatigue was encountered, and
one day a foot-soldier, calling to a horseman who was his
friend, drew forth from his wallet a linen bag in which were
six pounds of pearls, probably filched from one of the Indian
sepulchres. These he offered as a gift to his comrade, being
heartily tired of carrying them on his back, though he had a
pair of broad shoulders capable of bearing the burden of
a mule. The horseman refused to accept so thoughtless
an offer. "Keep them yourself," said he, "you have most
need of them. The Governor intends shortly to send messengers to Havana; you can forward these presents and have
them sold, and three or four horses and mules purchased for
you with the proceeds, so that you need no longer go on
foot."

Juan Terron was piqued at having his offer refused.

"Well," said he, "if you will not have them, I swear I will not carry them, and they shall remain here." So saying, he untied the bag, and, whirling around, as if he were sowing seed, scattered the pearls in all directions among the thickets and herbage. Then putting up the bag in his wallet, as if it were more valuable than the pearls, he marched on, leaving his comrades and the other by-standers astonished at his folly.

The soldiers made a hasty search for the scattered pearls and recovered thirty of them. When they beheld their great size and beauty, none of them being bored and discolored, they lamented that so many of them had been lost; for the whole would have sold in Spain for more than six thousand ducats. This egregious folly gave rise to a common proverb in the army, that "There are no pearls for Juan Terron." The poor fellow himself became an object of constant jest and ridicule, until, at last, made sensible of his absurd conduct, he implored them never to banter him further on the subject.

After a march of five days the army reached Guaxule. Upon the route, both men and horses had suffered from an insufficient supply of maize and of meat. When within half a league of the chief town of the province, De Soto was met by the Cacique or King, escorted by a band of five hundred warriors attired in decorated mantles of various skins, and adorned with feathers of brilliant hues. The interview was entirely amicable; and by him and his train was the Governor conducted to the village consisting of three hundred houses. It occupied a pleasant situation and was well watered by streams taking their rise in the adjacent mountains. The Adelantado was hospitably entertained at the dwelling of the Mico, which stood upon the top of an artificial elevation "surrounded by a terrace wide enough

for six men to go abreast." The site of Guaxule we believe
to be identical, or very nearly so, with *Coosawattee Old
Town*, in the southeastern corner of Murray county.

Perceiving that the Christians were killing and eating the
village dogs, the native King collected and presented three
hundred of them to the Spaniards. This animal was not
used as an article of food by the Aborigines. On the contrary, it was held in special regard. The constant companion of its master in his journeys through the forests, and
in hunting and fishing,—a trusted guard about his camp-
fires and at the door of the home lodge,—not infrequently
were accorded to it rites of sepulture akin to those with
which the owner was complimented. We wonder therefore
at this gift, and are inclined to interpret it rather as a
euphemistic statement that these dogs were appropriated by
the strangers.

Four days were here passed by the command. An Indian
was dispatched with a message to the Chief of Chiaha re-
questing that he would concentrate maize at that place, as it
was the purpose of the Governor to tarry some time in that
village.

After two days' travel the town of Canasagua was reached.
There is no good reason why we should not recognize in this
name the original of that borne at the present day by the
river Connasauga. This stage in the journey of De Soto we
locate at or near the junction of the Connasauga and Coosawattee rivers, in originally Cass, now Gordon county.
Before reaching this town he was met by twenty men from
the village, each bearing a basket of mulberries. This fruit
was here abundant and well flavored. Plums and walnut
trees were growing luxuriantly throughout the country, at-
taining a size and beauty, without planting or pruning,
which could not be surpassed in the irrigated and well culti-
vated gardens of Spain.

Following the course of the Oostanaula, and marching well nigh parallel with its left bank, the army moved in the direction of Chiaha [Ychiaha, Ichiaha, China]. On the fifth day, when within two leagues of that town, fifteen Indians, bearing presents of maize, met the Adelantado. They conveyed the salutations of the Cacique, and a message that he was in his village awaiting the arrival of the strangers. They further assured the Governor that twenty barbacoas, full of maize, were there subject to his orders. Chiaha was entered by the Spaniards on the fifth of June. Cordially was De Soto welcomed by the Cacique, who resigned to him the use and occupancy of his residence. Into his mouth the Gentleman of Elvas puts the following address :

" *Powerful and Excellent Master :*

"Fortunate am I that you will make use of my services. Nothing could happen that would give me so great contentment, or which I should value more. From Guaxule you sent to have maize for you in readiness to last two months : you have in this town twenty barbacoas full of the choicest and best to be found in all this country. If the reception I give is not worthy so great a prince, consider my youth, which will relieve me of blame, and receive my good will which, with true loyalty and pure, shall ever be shown in all things that concern your welfare."

To these words the Governor responded feelingly, assuring the young Chief that he was greatly pleased with his gifts and kindness, and that he would always regard him as a brother.

De Soto had now reached the confluence of the Etowah and the Oostenaula rivers. The ancient village of Chiaha has been supplanted by the modern city of Rome. The town is described as situated between two arms of a river

and seated near one of them. Both branches were then
fordable, and the meadow lands adjacent to their banks were
rich. Maize fields appeared on every hand. There was
an abundance of lard in calabashes, which the inhabitants
said was prepared from bear's fat. Oil of walnuts, "clear
and of good taste," was found in the possession of the
natives. They also had a honey-comb which the Christians
had never seen before. It was a pleasant and hospitable
region, and the army here rested for thirty days. The
horses had become so jaded by rough and continuous
marches, and so enfeebled from lack of substantial food,
that it was absolutely necessary to indulge them in a season
of quiet. When they arrived at Chiaha they were so worn
out that they could not carry their riders. They were ac-
cordingly turned out to graze. So amiable were the natives,
that although greatly exposed, the Spaniards suffered no
molestation from them either in their persons or animals.
Had they, in their unguarded condition, seen fit to set upon
the Christians they would have been in a bad way to have
defended themselves. Contrary to the conduct of the
natives on similar occasions in other localities, the inhabitants of Chiaha did not abandon their houses upon the
approach of the army, or during the sojourn of the Spaniards. Consequently, the soldiers were quartered beneath
the trees:—the only house occupied by a European being
that of the Chief, in which the Governor lodged.

In response to his repeated inquiries in regard to gold,
De Soto was here informed that to the north, and in a
province called Chisca, were mines of copper, and of a
metal of like color, but finer and brighter. Encouraged by
this information, confirmatory of what he had been told at
Cutifachiqui, he dispatched Juan de Villalobos and Fran-
cisco de Silvera,—two brave soldiers who volunteered for

the enterprise,—to proceed on foot and, if possible, locate these mines.

After an absence of ten days they returned and reported that they had been well received by the natives: that their route lay partly through land excellent for grain and pasturage, and again over mountains so rugged that it would not be practicable for the army to cross them: that they had found among the natives a buffalo hide, an inch thick and with hair as soft as sheep's wool; and lastly, that they had seen only a fine variety of copper, such as had already been met with. From the appearance of the soil, however, they thought it not improbable that both gold and silver were native to the region.

While De Soto was awaiting the return of these soldiers, the Cacique of Chiaha one day presented him with a string of pearls two arms in length. These pearls were as large as filberts; and, had they not been perforated, would have been of great value. Thankfully receiving them, De Soto complimented the Indian with pieces of velvet and cloths of various colors, and with other Spanish trifles held in much esteem by the natives. Upon inquiry, he learned that these pearls had been obtained in the neighborhood, and that in the sepulchres of the ancestors of the Cacique many were stored. The Governor being curious to see in what manner these pearls were extracted from the shells, the Cacique dispatched forty canoes to fish for the oysters during the night. "At an early hour next morning a quantity of wood was gathered and piled up on the banks of the river, and being set on fire was speedily reduced to glowing coals. As soon as the canoes arrived, the coals were spread out and the oysters were laid upon them. They soon opened with the heat, and from some of the first thus opened, the Indians obtained ten or twelve pearls as large as peas, which they brought to the Governor and Cacique, who were standing together looking on. The pearls were of a fine quality, but somewhat discolored by the fire and smoke. The Indians were prone also to injure these pearls by boring them with a heated copper instrument.

" De Soto having gratified his curiosity, returned to his quarters to partake of the morning meal. While eating, a soldier entered with a large pearl in his hand. He had stewed some oysters, and, in eating them, felt this pearl between his teeth. Not having been injured by fire or smoke, it retained its beautiful whiteness, and was so large and perfect in its form that several Spaniards, who pretended to be skilled in these matters, declared it would be worth four hundred ducats in Spain. The soldier would have given it to the Governor to present to his wife,—Doña Isabel de Bobadilla,—but De Soto declined the generous offer, advising the soldier to preserve it until he got to Havana, where he might purchase horses and many other things with it ; moreover, in reward of his liberal disposition, De Soto insisted upon paying the fifth of the value, due to the Crown."

The mussel or oyster here alluded to was doubtless the pearl-bearing unio still native to the Etowah and the Oostanaula, and to many other southern streams. At that early period these shells were far more numerous than they are at present. Artificial shell heaps still attest how industriously in that olden time these margatiferous shells were collected by primitive peoples, who valued them not only for their flesh, but also for the glistening beads they contained, and for their iridescent coverings from which various ornaments were manufactured. When pounded they were kneaded with clay and tended materially to give consistency and strength to the pottery of the region.

The denudation of the banks of these streams, and the destruction of extensive forests in reducing wild lands to a state of cultivation, have caused marked changes in the animal life of the country.

> "Before these fields were shorn and tilled,
> Full to the brim our rivers flowed."

Limpid then, with constant volumes they pursued their accustomed channels. Subsequently, becoming turbid with the soil washed from the slopes of a hundred hills, and no longer fed with regularity by well shaded and pure springs, but at one time enfeebled by drought and at another engorged by torrents, these streams have, for many years, been liable to sudden and violent fluctuations. Multitudes of margatiferous unios have consequently been torn from their habitats by unruly currents, and imbedded beyond life in sand bars and muddy deposits. The stable bottoms upon which they rested and multiplied have been rendered both uncertain and unwholesome; and thus it has come to pass that a marked extinction of such animal life has ensued.

A melancholy occurrence which took place while the army was at Chiaha is thus narrated by Theodore Irving in his "Conquest of Florida:"

"A cavalier, one Luis Bravo de Xeres, strolling, with lance in hand, along a plain bordering on the river, saw a small animal at a short distance, and launched his weapon at it. The lance missed the mark; but, slipping along the grass, shot over the river bank. Luis Bravo ran to recover his lance, but to his horror found it had killed a Spaniard who had been fishing with a reed on the margin of the river at the foot of the bank. The steel point of the lance had entered one temple and come out at the other, and the poor Spaniard had dropped dead on the spot. His name was Juan Mateos; he was the only one in the expedition that had gray hairs, from which circumstance he was universally called father Mateos, and respected as such. His unfortunate death was lamented by the whole army."

A month had well nigh elapsed since the arrival of the Spaniards at Chiaha. The men were entirely rested and the horses were again in good order. The Governor resolved to take up the line of march for Coça on the Coosa river. Before leaving, yielding to the importunity of some in his command "who wanted more than was in reason," he asked from the Cacique thirty women, that he might take them with him in the capacity of slaves. The Chief responded that he would consult with his principal men. Informed of the demand, and before answer had been made to it, the inhabitants fled by night from the town, taking their women and children with them. Although the Cacique professed his regret at the course his people had pursued, and acknowledged his inability to control them, the Governor, with thirty mounted men and as many foot soldiers, went in pursuit of the fugitives. In passing the towns of some of the chiefs who had absconded, he cut down and destroyed their maize fields. Proceeding along up the stream he found the natives congregated upon an island in the river to which his cavalry could not penetrate. By an Indian he sent them word that if they would return and furnish him with some tamemes, he would not disturb their women, seeing in what special affection they were held. Upon this assurance they all came back to their homes.

Parting from the Cacique of Chiaha with kind words, and having received from him some slaves as a gift, De Soto set out with his companions down the valley of the Coosa, and was soon, without further incident of moment, beyond the confines of the present State of Georgia. He had entered this territory early in March, 1540, and departed from it on the second day of July in the same year.

Thus did these mail-clad Spaniards,—the first Europeans who traversed the soil of Georgia, beheld the primal beauties of her forests, rivers, plains, and mountains, participated in the hospitalities of her primitive peoples, and sought but found not the treasures hidden within her bosom,—disappointed, yet not despairing, pass onward in quest of richer native lords and goodlier countries.

We may not follow them even until that near day when, amid the smoke and thunder of battle at Mauvila, they barely escaped destruction at the hands of the lion-hearted Alibamons. It lies not within our purpose to accompany them as, impeded by tangled brake, morass, and stream, often pinched by hunger, frequently opposed by the Red Warriors, now buoyed up by hope, again oppressed by apprehension, they painfully groped their way through vast and unknown regions this side and even beyond the Meschachepi. In the end, their golden visions vanished, the body of their leader silently and in darkness entombed in the *Father of Waters*, few in numbers and broken in spirit, their munitions exhausted, the survivors of this famous expedition fled from the land wherein they had garnered a harvest only of privation, peril, sorrow, mortification and death.

APPENDIX.

March 3, 1540.—Left Anhaica [Tallahassee, Fla.?]

March 7, 1540.—Crossed a deep river [Oclockony?]

March 9, 1540.—Arrived at Capachiqui.

March 21, 1540.—Came to Toalli.

March 24, 1540.—Left Toalli.

March 25, 1540.—Arrived at Achese.

April 1, 1540.—Departed from Achese.

April 4, 1540.—Passed through the town of Altamaca.

April 10, 1540.—Arrived at Ocute.

April 12, 1540.—Left Ocute.

Passed through a town whose lord was called Cofaqui, and came to the province of another lord named Patofa.

April 14, 1540.—Departed from Patofa.

April 20, 1540.—Lost in a pine barren. Six days consumed in fording two rivers and in the effort to find a way of escape.

April 26, 1540.—Set out for Aymay.

Reached Aymay before nightfall.

April 28, 1540.—Departed for Cutifachiqui.

May 3, 1540.—Left Cutifachiqui.

May 10, 1540.—Arrived at Chelaque.

May 15, 1540.—Arrived at Xualla.

May 20, 1540.—Arrived at Guaxule.

May 22, 1540.—Arrived at Canasagua.

June 5, 1540.—Arrived at Chiaha.

July 1, 1540.—Departed from Chiaha.

www.ingramcontent.com/pod-product-compliance
Lightning Source LLC
Chambersburg PA
CBHW021600270326
41931CB00009B/1316